GORDON RAMSAY

Pasta Sauces

Photography by SIMON WHEELER

THE MASTER CHEFS

TED SMART

GORDON RAMSAY embarked on a career in professional soccer with Glasgow Rangers; when he gave up football and turned to cooking, he moved to London and began working for Marco Pierre White. He also cooked at Le Gavroche in London before spending two and a half years in Paris, under Guy Savoy and Joel Robuchon.

After his years working amid a constellation of Michelin stars, at the age of 26 he returned to London to open his own restaurant, Aubergine, in October 1993. His light, subtle and sophisticated cooking earned him his first Michelin star in 1995.

He has appeared on a number of TV programmes, including BBC2's *Food and Drink*, and his book, *A Passion for Flavour*, was published in September 1996.

CONTENTS

For me, the most important element in a dish is flavour. Presentation may give instant pleasure, but a great taste holds the memory.

INTRODUCTION

There is a great sense of excitement with pasta dishes: they are almost infinitely variable and it's easy to make them very much your own. In these recipes, I've created a selection of subtle and unusual sauces for pasta. My style derives from a classical French training, so many of my recipes have a base of well-flavoured stock, which makes them lighter than those based solely on cloying cream or butter, or heavy and acidic canned tomatoes.

Lighter sauces are best served with thin pastas such as spaghetti, creamy sauces with thicker, flatter pastas such as tagliatelle or shapes that have hollows to capture the sauce.

Buy good-quality fresh or dried pasta made with 100% durum (hard) wheat that has a good texture, remaining *al dente* (still firm to the bite) even if slightly overcooked. Better still, make your own – it's not difficult, you just need a little practice. I love making fresh pasta; it happens twice a day in my restaurant.

Each of these recipes makes enough sauce for four people, allowing about 50–75 g/2–3 oz dried or 75–100 g/3–3½ oz fresh pasta per person.

SWEET PEPPER SAUCE
with clams

500 G/1 LB 2 OZ FRESH CLAMS (OR
    MUSSELS) IN THEIR SHELLS,
    THOROUGHLY SCRUBBED
1 LARGE BOUQUET GARNI OF
    FRESH HERBS
300 ML/½ PINT DRY WHITE WINE
50 G/2 OZ BUTTER
2 RED PEPPERS, SEEDED AND FINELY
    CHOPPED
2 YELLOW PEPPERS, SEEDED AND
    FINELY CHOPPED
6 SHALLOTS, FINELY CHOPPED
1 SPRIG EACH OF TARRAGON,
    CHERVIL AND THYME
1 FRESH BAY LEAF
3 TABLESPOONS DRY VERMOUTH
2 TEASPOONS WHITE WINE VINEGAR
SEA SALT AND FRESHLY GROUND
    BLACK PEPPER
1 TABLESPOON CHOPPED FRESH
    BASIL

SERVES 4

Rinse the clams two or three times in cold water, then place in a saucepan with the bouquet garni and white wine. Cover and cook over a medium heat for about 5 minutes, shaking the pan occasionally. Drain the clams through a muslin-lined sieve, reserving the cooking liquid. Discard any clams that have not opened. Remove most of the clams from their shells and reserve, discarding the empty shells.

Melt half the butter in a saucepan and gently fry the chopped peppers and shallots with the herbs for about 10 minutes or until softened.

Add the vermouth and cook, uncovered, for about 3 minutes or until reduced, then add the vinegar and cook for a further 1 minute or until evaporated.

Add the reserved clam cooking liquid and simmer, uncovered, for about 10 minutes. Remove the herb sprigs.

The sauce can be left chunky with pieces of pepper or, if you prefer a smooth sauce, tip the contents of the pan into a liquidizer or food processor and purée, then rub through a sieve.

Season to taste, then add the clams, reheat and briskly stir in the remaining butter. Toss with freshly cooked pasta and serve at once, sprinkled with the basil.

SAFFRON VELOUTÉ
with scallops

4 SHALLOTS, THINLY SLICED
15 G/½ OZ UNSALTED BUTTER
½ TEASPOON SAFFRON STRANDS
250 ML/8 FL OZ DRY WHITE WINE
250 ML/8 FL OZ DRY VERMOUTH
500 ML/16 FL OZ FISH, VEGETABLE
   OR CHICKEN STOCK
   (PAGES 28–29)
SEA SALT AND FRESHLY GROUND
   BLACK PEPPER
250 ML/8 FL OZ DOUBLE CREAM
250 ML/8 FL OZ SINGLE CREAM

TO SERVE

4–12 SCALLOPS (DEPENDING ON
   SIZE)
1 TABLESPOON CHOPPED CHERVIL

SERVES 4

In a wide saucepan, gently cook the shallots with the butter for about 5 minutes, then crush in the saffron strands and continue cooking very, very gently for another 5 minutes.

Stir in the wine and vermouth and simmer, uncovered, until the liquid has reduced down to a thin syrupy glaze, about 10 minutes. Add the stock and simmer until reduced by half. Season to taste.

Stir in the two creams and simmer, still uncovered, for about 10 minutes or until the consistency is smooth and velvety.

Meanwhile, steam the scallops or sear in a hot nonstick pan.

Strain the sauce through a fine sieve, then toss with freshly cooked tagliatelle. Serve at once, with the scallops, sprinkled with the chervil.

Salmon or another fish can be used instead of the scallops.

TOMATO AND CARDAMOM COULIS
with vegetable brunoise

2 SHALLOTS, SLICED

1 GARLIC CLOVE, PEELED AND LEFT
WHOLE

8 TABLESPOONS OLIVE OIL

4 CARDAMOM PODS, SPLIT

1 SPRIG EACH OF THYME, BASIL AND
TARRAGON

3 TABLESPOONS DRY WHITE WINE

500 G/1 LB 2 OZ RIPE PLUM
TOMATOES, SKINNED AND
CHOPPED

1 TABLESPOON TOMATO PURÉE

SEA SALT AND FRESHLY GROUND
BLACK PEPPER

VEGETABLE BRUNOISE

1 SMALL AUBERGINE

1 YELLOW PEPPER

2 SMALL COURGETTES

SERVES 4

Put the shallots and garlic into a
saucepan with 2 tablespoons of the
oil. Cover and cook over a low
heat for 5 minutes, then add the
cardamom pods and herbs and
cook for a further 2 minutes.

Stir in the wine and cook for
1–2 minutes, until it evaporates,
then mix in the chopped tomatoes
and tomato purée. Season well,
then cover and simmer very gently
for about 15 minutes.

Meanwhile, cut the aubergine,
pepper and courgettes into large
dice. Heat 2 tablespoons of the oil
in a large frying pan and fry the
aubergine for 5–7 minutes or until
almost tender. Add the pepper and
courgette dice and continue to fry,
stirring frequently, for a further
5–7 minutes; they should be hot
through but should remain firm.

Remove the garlic clove from
the tomato mixture, then purée the
mixture with the remaining oil in
a liquidizer or food processor. Rub
the purée through a fine sieve,
season to taste and serve with
freshly cooked tagliatelle, sprinkled
with the vegetable brunoise.

PARSLEY CREAM SAUCE

100 G/3½ OZ CURLY LEAF PARSLEY
100 G/3½ OZ WATERCRESS
4 TABLESPOONS DOUBLE CREAM
SEA SALT AND FRESHLY GROUND
    BLACK PEPPER
ABOUT 200 ML/7 FL OZ CHICKEN
    OR VEGETABLE STOCK
    (PAGES 28–29)
CRISP FRIED CELERIAC
    (PAGE 29), TO GARNISH

SERVES 4

Wash the parsley and watercress thoroughly. Pick off and discard the thick stalks. Drain well.

Blanch the parsley in a large saucepan of boiling water for 4 minutes, then add the watercress and continue cooking for a further 1–2 minutes.

Drain well in a sieve, then tip the blanched leaves into an old, clean tea towel. Roll up and squeeze the towel tightly to extract all the water.

Place the leaves in a food processor with the cream and seasoning and blend to a smooth purée, scraping down the sides frequently. The secret of this sauce is to run the machine until the parsley and watercress become very smooth and glossy. When the consistency is quite silky, blend in the stock and return the sauce to the saucepan.

Return to a gentle boil for 1–2 minutes, taste and adjust the seasoning if required, then toss with freshly cooked pasta. Serve at once, garnished with crisp celeriac.

ROSEMARY CREAM SAUCE
with beans, bacon and asparagus

1 LITRE/1¾ PINTS CHICKEN STOCK
  (PAGE 28)
150 ML/¼ PINT DOUBLE CREAM
1 TEASPOON CHOPPED FRESH
  ROSEMARY
150 G/5 OZ ASPARAGUS TIPS
175 G/6 OZ LEAN BACON,
  IN ONE PIECE
1 TABLESPOON OLIVE OIL
200 G/7 OZ COOKED WHITE
  HARICOT OR CANNELLINI BEANS
SEA SALT AND FRESHLY GROUND
  BLACK PEPPER

SERVES 4

Put the stock in a saucepan and boil to reduce by half. Add the cream and rosemary and continue boiling until reduced to about 500 ml/16 fl oz. Remove from the heat and set aside.

Meanwhile, blanch the asparagus tips in boiling water for 2 minutes. Drain and rinse in cold running water. Drain well.

Cut the bacon into dice or narrow strips. Heat the oil in a frying pan and, when hot, fry the bacon, stirring occasionally, until golden brown and crisp. Drain on paper towels.

Return the sauce to a medium heat and stir in the white beans and half the crisp bacon. Simmer for 1–2 minutes, then taste and adjust the seasoning if required. Toss with freshly cooked pasta and serve at once, sprinkled with the asparagus tips and the remaining crisp bacon.

SAUCE ANTIBOISE

3 LARGE PLUM TOMATOES

200 ML/7 FL OZ OLIVE OIL

3 LARGE SHALLOTS, FINELY
    CHOPPED

2 GARLIC CLOVES, CRUSHED

6 LARGE FRESH BASIL LEAVES

2 SPRIGS OF CORIANDER

3 SPRIGS OF TARRAGON

1 TABLESPOON FRESH LEMON JUICE

SEA SALT AND FRESHLY GROUND
    BLACK PEPPER

SERVES 4

Score the base of each tomato with a sharp knife, place in a bowl and cover with boiling water. Leave for about 1 minute. Drain and rinse in cold water, then slip off the skins. Quarter the tomatoes, remove the seeds and cores and chop the flesh into fine dice. Set aside.

Heat the oil in a saucepan over low heat and cook the shallots and garlic for about 5 minutes or until softened. Remove from the heat.

Meanwhile, remove the stalks from the herbs if necessary; cut the leaves into thin julienne strips. Stir into the shallots and oil and leave to infuse for 5 minutes, then mix in the tomato dice.

Return to the heat and heat gently until piping hot. Add the lemon juice, season to taste, then toss with freshly cooked spaghetti.

WHITE BEAN CAPPUCCINO

500 ML/16 FL OZ CHICKEN OR
    VEGETABLE STOCK (PAGES 28–29)
250 G/9 OZ COOKED WHITE
    HARICOT OR CANNELLINI BEANS
150 ML/¼ PINT DOUBLE CREAM
2 TEASPOONS TRUFFLE OIL
SEA SALT AND FRESHLY GROUND
    BLACK PEPPER
15 G/½ OZ ICE-COLD BUTTER, CUT
    INTO SMALL PIECES
1 TABLESPOON CHOPPED FRESH
    CHIVES
SPRIGS OF CHERVIL

*This sauce is designed to go with
ravioli or cannelloni. Buy or make
your own favourite ravioli, or make
fresh lasagne pasta (page 30),
blanch, drain well and roll around
one of the following fillings:*
* *ratatouille*
* *blanched baby spinach leaves with
  fried, sliced mushrooms*
* *flaked white crab meat mixed with
  flaked cooked salmon, moistened
  with a little cream*
* *shredded cooked pheasant mixed
  with finely shredded, sautéed
  Savoy cabbage*

SERVES 4

Boil the stock until reduced to
about 300 ml/½ pint.

Meanwhile, purée the beans in
a liquidizer or food processor, then
scrape into a bowl. Using a hand-
held multi-blender, slowly whisk in
the stock, cream and truffle oil.
Season to taste, then pour the
sauce into a saucepan.

When ready to serve, place
your ravioli or cannelloni on four
warmed plates. Return the sauce
to a gentle boil and whisk back to
a froth with the hand-held blender.
While you whisk, add the pieces of
ice-cold butter – this helps to
stabilize the foam.

Spoon the top of the foam over
the pasta, continuing to reheat and
whisk the sauce as you serve.
Garnish with chives and chervil.

LEMONGRASS PRIMAVERA SAUCE

2 STALKS OF FRESH LEMONGRASS
125 ML/4 FL OZ OLIVE OIL
100 G/3½ OZ FINE GREEN BEANS
3 TABLESPOONS FRESH YOUNG PEAS
4 PLUM TOMATOES
1 SHALLOT, FINELY CHOPPED
GRATED RIND OF 1 SMALL LEMON
SQUEEZE OF FRESH LEMON JUICE
SEA SALT AND FRESHLY GROUND
    BLACK PEPPER
FINELY CHOPPED STONED BLACK
    OLIVES, TO GARNISH

SERVES 4

Trim the lemongrass, then cut in half lengthways. Slice finely and place in a saucepan with the oil; heat slowly until hot but not boiling. Remove from the heat and leave to infuse for about 5 minutes.

Meanwhile, trim the beans and cut into 2.5 cm/1 inch lengths. Blanch in boiling water for 2 minutes, then add the peas and cook for another minute. Drain and rinse in cold running water. Drain and dry on paper towels.

Score the base of each tomato with a sharp knife, place in a bowl and cover with boiling water. Leave for about 1 minute. Drain and rinse in cold water, then slip off the skins. Quarter the tomatoes, remove the seeds and cores and cut the flesh into fine dice.

Strain the infused oil through a sieve and discard the lemongrass.

Mix the oil with the shallot, lemon rind and juice and the beans, peas and diced tomatoes; season to taste. Toss with freshly cooked pasta and serve at once, as a warm salad, garnished with chopped black olives.

GLAZED BABY ONIONS
and light curry sauce

ABOUT 24 BABY ONIONS OR SMALL
    SHALLOTS, UNPEELED
200 G/7 OZ CARROTS, CUT INTO
    THIN BATONS OR JULIENNE
    STRIPS
25 G/1 OZ BUTTER
1 TABLESPOON OLIVE OIL
200 ML/7 FL OZ SWEET WHITE
    WINE
200 ML/7 FL OZ CHICKEN OR
    VEGETABLE STOCK (PAGES 28–29)
1 TEASPOON MILD CURRY PASTE
3 TABLESPOONS DOUBLE CREAM
100 G/3½ OZ YOUNG SPINACH
    LEAVES
SEA SALT AND FRESHLY GROUND
    BLACK PEPPER

SERVES 3–4

Blanch the onions or shallots
briefly in boiling water, then drain
and skin (blanching makes them
easier to peel). Blanch the carrots
in boiling water for 2 minutes,
then drain and set aside.

Heat the butter and oil in a
sauté pan and gently fry the onions
or shallots for about 10 minutes,
shaking the pan occasionally, until
softened and golden brown.

In a saucepan, boil the wine
until reduced by half, then add the
stock and curry paste and boil
again until reduced to about
300 ml/½ pint. Stir in the cream
and cook for 2 minutes.

Remove any thick stalks from
the spinach leaves and add to the
sauce, stirring until just wilted. Add
the onions and carrots, then season
to taste. Toss with freshly cooked
pasta and serve at once.

WILD MUSHROOM SAUCE

100 G/3½ OZ SELECTION OF WILD
  MUSHROOMS
100 G/3½ OZ BUTTON
  MUSHROOMS
3 TABLESPOONS OLIVE OIL
1 TABLESPOON FRESH LEMON JUICE
SEA SALT AND FRESHLY GROUND
  BLACK PEPPER
VELOUTÉ SAUCE, OMITTING
  SAFFRON (PAGE 10)
FLAT-LEAF PARSLEY, TO GARNISH

SERVES 4

Pick over the wild mushrooms and
wipe clean with a damp cloth if
necessary. Chop both wild and
button mushrooms very finely.

Place the chopped mushrooms
in a wide shallow saucepan with
the oil and cook gently until liquid
starts to seep out. Add the lemon
juice and seasoning and cook
gently, stirring occasionally, until
the liquid has evaporated away. This
may take 20–30 minutes.

Bring the velouté sauce to
simmering point and stir in the
mushroom mixture. Taste and
adjust the seasoning if required.
Toss with freshly cooked pasta and
serve at once, garnished with flat-
leaf parsley.

THE BASICS

CHICKEN STOCK

ABOUT 1.5 KG/3 LB CHICKEN
    CARCASSES OR WINGS
2 STICKS OF CELERY, CHOPPED
1 LEEK, CHOPPED
1 LARGE ONION, QUARTERED
1 LARGE CARROT, CHOPPED
4 GARLIC CLOVES, UNPEELED
1 SPRIG OF THYME
1 TABLESPOON ROCK SALT

MAKES 2 LITRES/3½ PINTS
Put all the ingredients into a
stockpot with 2.5 litres/4½ pints
cold water. Bring to the boil, then
partially cover the pan and simmer
for about 3 hours, skimming
occasionally.

Pour through a muslin-lined
sieve into a large bowl. Leave to
cool, then chill.

FISH STOCK

1 LEEK, CHOPPED
1 SMALL ONION, QUARTERED
1 STICK OF CELERY, CHOPPED
½ FENNEL BULB, SLICED
2 GARLIC CLOVES, UNPEELED
100 ML/3½ FL OZ OLIVE OIL
1.5 KG/3 LB WHITE FISH BONES,
    CHOPPED
300 ML/½ PINT DRY WHITE WINE
1 LARGE BOUQUET GARNI OF
    FRESH HERBS
½ LEMON, SLICED
¼ TEASPOON WHITE PEPPERCORNS

MAKES 2 LITRES/3½ PINTS
Put all the ingredients into a
stockpot with 2 litres/3½ pints
cold water. Bring to the boil, then
simmer, uncovered, for 20 minutes,
skimming occasionally.

Remove from the heat and
leave to stand for 10 minutes, then
strain through a muslin-lined sieve
into a large bowl.

VEGETABLE STOCK

3 ONIONS
1 LEEK
2 STICKS OF CELERY
6 CARROTS
1 WHOLE HEAD OF GARLIC, SLIT IN
    HALF
1 LEMON, SLICED
¼ TEASPOON WHITE PEPPERCORNS
1 SMALL BAY LEAF
4 STAR ANISE
SPRIG EACH OF TARRAGON, BASIL,
    CORIANDER, THYME, PARSLEY
    AND CHERVIL
200 ML/7 FL OZ DRY WHITE WINE

MAKES 1.5 LITRES/2½ PINTS
Put all the ingredients, except the herbs and wine, into a stockpot with 2 litres/3½ pints cold water. Bring to the boil, then simmer gently for 10 minutes.

Remove from the heat, add the herbs and wine and leave to infuse until cool.

Chill in the refrigerator for 24 hours, with all the vegetables, then strain through a muslin-lined sieve into a large bowl.

PASTA GARNISHES

- wafer-thin shavings of fresh Parmesan or pecorino cheese
- chopped fresh herbs (parsley, chervil, dill, basil, coriander)
- a concassé of finely chopped olives mixed with finely diced skinned tomatoes
- julienne strips of Parma ham
- crisp-fried vegetables (celeriac, beetroot, carrot, whole baby spinach leaves). Cut root vegetables first into thin slices, then into fine julienne strips. Leave to dry on paper towels for 20 minutes.
  Shallow fry the vegetable strips or whole spinach leaves in hot olive oil to cover for 3–5 minutes or until cooked but not coloured. Drain on paper towels placed on a baking sheet.
  Heat the oven to its lowest setting and dry the shredded vegetables in the oven, with the door slightly open, until crisp but not browned. Change the paper towels once or twice during this drying-out period.

MAKING FRESH PASTA

You will need a pasta rolling machine and a food processor

225 G/8 OZ PLAIN FLOUR
GOOD PINCH OF SEA SALT
2 EGGS (SIZE 2)
3 EGG YOLKS
1 TABLESPOON OLIVE OIL

Sift the flour and salt together, then place in a food processor with the remaining ingredients and process until the mixture forms coarse crumbs. Test the texture by pressing a small amount between your finger and thumb. If it cracks, then process for a few more seconds.

Tip the mixture on to a work surface and knead until you have a ball of smooth dough that feels soft but not sticky. Wrap in clingfilm and leave to rest for an hour or so.

Divide the dough into large walnut-size balls and feed through a pasta rolling machine several times, according to the manufacturer's instructions, until you have long, thin sheets of pasta.

For lasagne or cannelloni, cut the sheets to the required lengths. For tagliatelle or spaghetti, cut each sheet into ribbons using the special machine cutters.

Blanch in boiling salted water for 30 seconds to 1 minute. Drain and plunge into ice-cold water. Drain again and set aside.

To serve, reheat in a little boiling water with a knob of butter for 1–2 minutes.

THE MASTER CHEFS

SOUPS
ARABELLA BOXER

MEZE, TAPAS AND ANTIPASTI
AGLAIA KREMEZI

PASTA SAUCES
GORDON RAMSAY

RISOTTO
MICHELE SCICOLONE

SALADS
CLARE CONNERY

MEDITERRANEAN
ANTONY WORRALL THOMPSON

VEGETABLES
PAUL GAYLER

LUNCHES
ALASTAIR LITTLE

COOKING FOR TWO
RICHARD OLNEY

FISH
RICK STEIN

CHICKEN
BRUNO LOUBET

SUPPERS
VALENTINA HARRIS

THE MAIN COURSE
ROGER VERGÉ

ROASTS
JANEEN SARLIN

WILD FOOD
ROWLEY LEIGH

PACIFIC
JILL DUPLEIX

CURRIES
PAT CHAPMAN

HOT AND SPICY
PAUL AND JEANNE RANKIN

THAI
JACKI PASSMORE

CHINESE
YAN-KIT SO

VEGETARIAN
KAREN LEE

DESSERTS
MICHEL ROUX

CAKES
CAROLE WALTER

COOKIES
ELINOR KLIVANS

THE MASTER CHEFS

This edition produced for The Book People Ltd,

Hall Wood Avenue, Haydock, St Helens WAII 9UL

First published in 1996 by

WEIDENFELD & NICOLSON

THE ORION PUBLISHING GROUP

ORION HOUSE

5 UPPER ST MARTIN'S LANE

LONDON WC2H 9EA

British Library Cataloguing-in-Publication data

A catalogue record for this book is available

from the British Library.

ISBN 0 297 83631 5

DESIGNED BY THE SENATE

EDITOR MAGGIE RAMSAY

FOOD STYLIST JOY DAVIES

ASSISTANT KATY HOLDER